JoVonna Williams
Single Mother Diagnosed and Conquered a Unique Disease

My name is JoVonna Williams and I am a single mother of three children. They include Cheyenne (my guardian angel) who would have been 16 and two boys; Demari who is 14 and Dominic who is 4 years old. I am a Christian who was born and raised in the church. Currently, I attend Oakland Church of Christ located in Southfield, MI. I have a seven year professional background working for a OB/GYN physician's private practice. I also have four years of experience in the auto finance industry where I worked in the repossession and garnishment departments.

Now I have a different part to my story I want to share. In 2010 at the age of 29, I was diagnosed with a rare condition *Eosinophilic Myenteric Ganglionitis,* which is an auto immune disorder that causes my colon and my bowel to attack one another. I have been told I am the fourth person in the world to be officially diagnosed with this disease. I was diagnosed at Cleveland Clinic Hospital after undergoing seven hours of surgery. I had a partial colectomy (removal of damaged colon), with a total rectal reconstruction and a temporary Ileostomy pouch which is a bag used to collect bowel contents. The surgery was a total success, but the recovery was rough and very painful. I was very sick and spent three weeks in the hospital, and I even lost thirty-seven pounds due to not being able to eat. Three months later, the pouch was permanently removed and reversed.

A year later I was blessed to have my second son. I was told I am the first person known to have a child diagnosed with my condition. The pregnancy was rough and I spent a lot of time in the hospital. Dominic was born a preemie almost five weeks early with no complications.

I have endured over 100 hospitalizations since being diagnosed. At one time, I was immobilized on my left-side from my waist down to my foot and loss total feeling in my left foot due to a side effect from a medication given. I spent four months in the hospital and weighed almost 200 pounds when I got out from being on steroids.

I had to temporarily live in a nursing home for complete physical therapy. I have been to several hospital facilities because the care has been either inadequate or just downright bad. I have been called a "drug seeking" person and many other things simply because the doctor's are practicing medicine and some have even become desensitized to patient needs. As a result, I am unable to work and I am on full disability.

I share my story to encourage, motivate, and uplift everyone I encounter being a testimony and a sense of hope. If I can help just one person then I feel all I have been through has a purpose. I can do all things through Christ who strengthen me (Philippians 4:13). Be encouraged and smile.

Charismata Homes is a nonprofit organization began five years ago, designed to help families in crisis. Charismata Homes was formed to specifically assist homeless mothers. Charismata is a valuable resource to help single mothers educate themselves about how manage as a single mother and navigate through daily living. We also assist them with their basic and more challenging needs.

Charismata provides mentor, educational, and parenting workshops. Clients are also granted furnished transitional housing.

Food Pantry: The food pantry is the *moms* hardship operation. The food pantry is one of the most progressive pantries in the area because of it's unique model. Guest to the pantry can visit every Tuesday, Thursday and Saturday with appointments only. Food is available to low income mothers and their children in the community. Food donations are needed to help build our pantry.

Personal Pantry: The personal pantry is available monthly on an emergency basis to assist mothers with the following personal items:

- Bar soap
- Laundry detergent
- Feminine hygiene products
- Toilet tissue

- Deodorant
- Shampoo
- Toothpaste

Emergency Baby Pantry: There is a constant need for items for emergency Baby Pantry such as diapers formula, baby wipes and newborn clothes. Other items include:

- Bottles
- Towels/washcloths
- Blankets
- Socks

Donation drop off:
Charismata Homes
18642 W Mcnichols
Detroit, MI 48219
Phone: (248) 773-2866

Clothes Closet: Gently used clothing, shoes and linens are provided to our mothers and children. Donations are needed.

PROVIDING HELP FOR THE COMMUNITY AND NEIGHBORHOODS

CHARISMATA

HOMES MAGAZINE

NEW TRANSITIONAL HOMES FOR BOYS IN DETROIT, MI

MICHIGAN MOTHER BATTLES A RARE DISEASE

PLUS MORE

THE LATEST TRENDS FOR HAIR AND NAILS

CHECK OUT THE NEWEST FASHION BOUTIQUES IN THE MIDWEST

Tez Rippa
RAP ARTIST/FIREMEN HEATS UP THE MIDWEST WITH A WHOLE NEW SOUND

Michelle Dixson
HELPING THE COMMUNITY WITH LOVE AND DEDICATION

US - $9.99

OCTOBER 2015 No. 2
WWW.CHARISMATAHOMESANDCOMPANY.COM

CHARISMATA HOMES MAGAZINE

3. JoVonna Williams
THE CHALLENGES OF BATTLING A RARE DISEASE AND RAISING A FAMILY.

9. Aries Closet
THE NEW FASHION MODEL THAT'S TAKING FASHION INTO THE NEXT GENERATION.

10. Treasures & Things Boutique
EXPERIENCE HOW TASHA WHITE TURNED HER BUSINESS INTO A VERY SPECIAL PLACE FOR HOMELESS AND BATTERED WOMEN TO FEEL BEAUTIFUL AGAIN.

11. Local Hair and Nail Stylist
LOCAL STYLIST MARIAH DIXSON IS BRINGING 2015 A WHOLE NEW LOOK TO MIDWEST MICHIGAN.

14. Rapper/Fireman
TEZ "MARTEZ DIXSON" RIPPA TALKS ABOUT HIS CAREER AS AN ARTIST AND FIREMAN.

CONTENT

Michelle Dixson
CEO - Charismata Homes, LLC

19. Michelle Dixson was born and raised in Detroit, MI. She was baptized at Westside Church of Christ at the age of 14. She is an active member of the Redford Church of Christ, where she has been a member for 16 years. One of her favorite scriptures is, "For I know the thoughts that I think toward you, saith the Lord, thoughts of peace, and not of evil, to give you an expected end" (Jeremiah 29:11).

Michelle was a single mother of four before God blessed her with a God-fearing husband, Roy, on March 28, 2004. God blessed them to adopt two additional children and also blessed them through their union with their own daughter, Morgan. They are the proud parents of seven children. They refer to their six girls as "Diamonds" and their son as the "Gem" of the family.

Michelle attended Sally Esser Beauty School and operated her own shop for five years. She also enrolled in a Child Psychology program at Henry Ford Community College. She continued her education at Northwest Christian Institute and received her Leadership Diploma in January 2008. She plans to continue her Christian education studies.

Michelle has been employed full-time at Sinai-Grace Hospital in Detroit, MI for the past 20 years. She currently works in the Admitting Department. She is the President/CEO for Charismata Homes & Company, a nonprofit organization for homeless single mothers.

Michelle wants God to continue to sustain her with strong, unwavering faith through everything in life. She recognizes that she cannot make it without His daily guidance.

Printed In The United States of America
Copyright © 2015. All Right Reserved.

Career Clothes Closet: Is to provide a interview outfit an to help women gain the professional clothing that they need for a job.

transitional living   daily rules

CHARISMATA HOMES

Founder | Director | Michelle Henry

CHARISMATA HOMES TRANSITIONAL LIVING

The Residential Transitional Living - A home where residents stabilize and learn independent living skills in a highly supervised environment.

The Supervised Housing Program

Our supported housing program offers both transitional living and long-term mental health residential opportunities as residents move toward greater levels of independence.

All residents can participate in our in-house Resident Recovery and Enrichment Program. This program provides opportunities to the residents to rediscover and pursue activities of interest, fitness, and independent living skill building.

Daily Rules for Transitional Living Program

Daily - Goals All residents must demonstrate they are following their case plan and making progress toward self-sufficiency.

Curfew - Residents must abide by the curfew for their status level.

School Staff - work with all residents on their educational goals, including return to high school, GED preparation, or college as appropriate.

Employment - If youth are not attending school, they must look for and obtain steady employment.

Housekeeping - residents are responsible for keeping their storage area neat, making the bed, storing belongings neatly, and removing trash from the area.

Meals - Charismata Staff is responsible for preparing meals.

transitional living

daily rules

Our diverse staff contributes to making Charismata Homes a warm, caring atmosphere where residents are supported and encouraged as they make progress.

As residents stabilize and build skills, they transition to our Supervised Housing Program. Many continue to progress and move out and live in their own apartment in the community. Some residents stay in our in-house programs on a long-term or permanent basis and continue to benefit from the support services provided.

Charismata Homes Transitional Living, promotes a resident's recovery through the individual's integration in the community.

- psychiatric providers & mental health centers

- medical treatment

- psychosocial rehabilitation programs

- vocational programs

- colleges and universities

- arts and music programs

- museums and theaters

- sports and sporting events

- restaurants, coffee houses, shopping and

- transportation

Laundry - Residents are responsible for doing their wash at a Laundromat each week or in house.

Cleaning & Maintenance - Residents are responsible for keeping their room and common areas clean and well-maintained.

Budget - As part of life skills training, residents with jobs must save 60% of their income. Residents prepare a budget with the case manager which includes transportation, clothing, personal products, and entertainment.
04\01\2014

Consequences for Rule Infractions

Residents who break curfew or violate other rules must deal with the consequences.

A range of consequences may be given, depending on the rule violation, severity of the infraction and repeat offenses.

Consequences include:

- the natural consequences for not doing something

- verbal warning

- written warning

- additional chores

- loss of privileges

- program fines

- move to a lower program status level

- program suspension (time varies)

- program termination

FEATURE

ARIES CLOSET
IS ONE OF THE HOTTEST BOUTIQUES IN MICHIGAN. SPECIALIZING IN THE MOST HIPPEST, FRESHEST, AND EXCLUSIVE CLOTHING YOU CAN CREATE EVERLASTING MEMORIES IN.
Styled by Aries Closet

Andrea McCray
Fashion Mogul/Model

Andrea McCray is the representation of a strong, black fashion entrepreneur. Like most mothers who put their dreams on pause to raise their children, Andrea let her children reach adulthood before she decided to attentively seek her dreams. She always had a passion for fashion that was blossomed by years of modeling and styling. It was only inevitable for her to create and polish her very own fashion boutique. Now in full effect Aries Closet is located at 21910 Greenfield Road #4, Oak Park, Michigan 48237. You can also go online to www.ariescloset.net to find more exclusive photos and the latest fashion.

FEATURE

T&T FASHION WORLD

T&T TREASURES AND THINGS BOUTIQUE IS NOT YOUR AVERAGE BOUTIQUE. T&T TREASURES BOUTIQUE IS THE FUTURE OF FASHION WHO PLANS TO EXPAND WORLDWIDE INTO THE NEXT FASHION WORLD.

Photography and Graphics by Darius Blackmon

Tasha White
Fashion Mogul

My goal is to become one of the world's most influential women in fashion. I have successfully established T&T Treasures and Things Boutique since April of 2011 with my best friend Toria Higgins. I dream to style homeless women, battered women, and women with love self-esteem. I understand that the beauty of boutique clothing is powerful and I am constantly empowered by my surroundings and people who have crossed my path. I am proud to have met Michelle Henry Dixson of *Charismata Homes*. She is a very humble person who loves to help people no matter what their situation is. Contact: (248) 508-2943 instagram: @tashaboss40

FEATURE

MARIAH DIXSON THE STYLIST
IS SHOWING THE WORLD THAT SHE HAS MULTIPLE SKILLS. A DOUBLE THREAT IN THE BEAUTY INDUSTRY, A HAIR AND NAIL STYLIST.

by Carol Dorsey

Mariah was born February 20, 1994 and raised in Detroit Michigan. She graduated from Farmington High School. Mariah continued her education at Paul Mitchell the School Michigan in Ster-

ling Heights, MI. Mariah understood from an early age that hair wasn't just an accessory, but that great hair is the key to feeling beautiful. Mariah specializes in nails, precision cutting and coloring, styling, and extensions with her artistic vision. She's always investing in her education in the beauty industry to master her many crafts and talents. She keeps up with the latest styles, techniques and trends as they appear on the fashion scene. It's her personal goal to continue to grow and excel in her craft and ultimately share all that she learns. Mariah continues to improve her skills through international training and classes. Mariah is constantly evolving in the beauty industry by learning in hope of inspiring others. Her mission is to teach workshops, become a network educator, and a traveling stylist. Mariah's goal is to travel around the world

Serving as a stylist to not only women, but men as well. In addition, Mariah is also a dedicated nail technician. She likes to think that being blesses with endowment of her many skills, are compliments of her personality. When you find yourself in Mariah's hands, you're promised an enjoyable, professional as well as unforgettable experience.

Mariah's goal is to travel around the world serving as a stylist to not only women, but men as well.

FEATURE

Martez Dixson (born 7/28/88), Music name Tez Rippa is an american Rapper from Detroit, Michigan. Tez is also an entrepreneur and a fireman from Detroit MI. He was born and raised in Detroit. Martez took his music serious in 2006. A talented artist as himself always knew he had skills to write 16 bars to a beat. Once he had saw how his music releases so much stress off his mind, he started to write more to clear his mind from everyday situations. Martez main goal is to take his music to a higher level. He also want to be a top artist in the industry and become an inspiration to our younger men. It's has been 8 years in the making and as a single father Martez has finally reach a point where he's comfortably discovered his purpose. While holding down a job as a fireman, Martez is going to push his music to the highest level Lord willing. Tez Rippa who is a part of RBBMG (RocBoi Music Group) is getting started and the main focus is to change his lifestyle. Martez is strongly driven and heavily determines to do so and his time is now! Also look out for his Clothing Line coming soon.

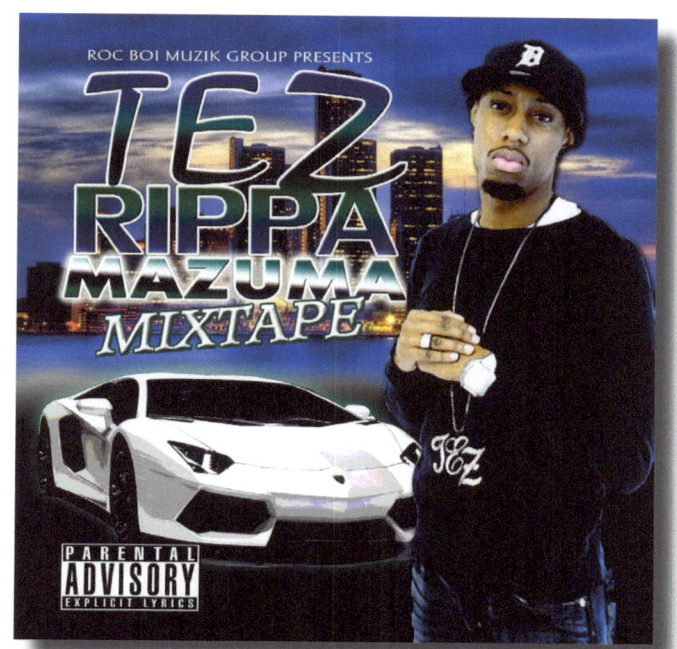

To download the Mixtape for FREE and for more information go to www.tezrippa.com.

Charismata PROGRAMS
ALL YEAR AROUND OUR PROGRAMS GIVE HOPE

One of the programs Charismata has been known for is the *Adopt a Family for Christmas Program.* During the second week of December, children and families receive gifts from generous members in our community.

Sinai-Grace Hospital Environmental Department adopted two families from our Charismata Homes program. Ms. Carter told her family that they wouldn't have a Christmas this year. Ms. Carter, is a mother with three children with financial challenges. The Carter family couldn't believe when they saw all the presents that were donated to her children. She had tears of joy in her eyes as we packed her car with gifts donated for her family. Charismata Homes and the Carter family like to give special thanks to Mr. Richard Kilgo, LC Bracey, and his staff for making this family's Christmas beautiful.

The Caleb family was also adopted for Christmas. This young lady is a mother of two twin girls and is currently expecting her third child. Sinai-Grace Environmental Department also adopted her family for Christmas. This courageous young lady knew she couldn't take care of her babies herself, especially when she had no source of income and no support system other then help from Charismata Homes program. Ms. Caleb loves her girls and would do anything to see them safe and properly cared for. When the young lady told me, "Mrs. Henry, I have no money to buy my girls gifts for Christmas and I feel less than a mother", I was speechless! I got a call next day from Richard Kilgo, asking if I had another family to adopt for Christmas. Richard and his staff did an outstanding job donating gifts for mom and her children. The Caleb family was Blessed with a lot of toys and gift cards. The Caleb family give special thanks to Richard and his staff.

We offer other progams, please visit our website if you would like to donate.
www.charismatahomes.com

who supported Charismata Homes.

Ada Jones
WA.AJONES LLC

LaToya Scott
DMC Employee

Pamela Evans
Sisters in Spirit Book Club

Angie Young
Miracles for Moms & Babes

Stephanie Day, Jamie Reed, Allisha Brown "Lee's Cakes", Shantel Minor
Redford Church of Christ, Elaine Lloyd, Barbra Westley, Officer Lee, Kimberly Ross
Evelyn D. Scott, Sonora Swann, Rochester Hills Fire Department, Sylvia Whittington
Connie McCullough, Alana Turner and Sinai-Grance Pharmacy Department

CHARISMATA HOMES BOARD MEMBERS

Theodora Knight
Vice President

Ronda Joiner
Treasurer

Menoriva Ross
Volunteer Coach/Mentor

Constance McCullough
Volunteer/Mentor

JoVonna Williams
Secretary

David Greenway
Media Designer

Casino Bailey
Website Designer

FOR DONATIONS PLEASE VISIT: WWW.CHARISMATAHOMESANDCOMPANY.COM

ASPIRE
THE BUSINESS OF BUSINESS

- List Your Company
- Attract More Customers
- Refer Other Members
- Earn 70% Commission

Become a member and save up to 50% on products and services from other members in the network.

Also earn cash by signing up other members. We offer our affiliates the highest earnings, up to 85% commission on each membership referral.

LIST YOUR BUSINESS FOR FREE LIMITED TIME OFFER!

THE BEST BUSINESS DIRECTORY IN THE WORLD.

visit us: www.aspirebiz2biz.com

COVER

MICHELLE DIXSON

THIS SUPERWOMAN REALLY LOVES TO HELP WOMEN AND CHILDREN. HER MISSION IS TO GET AS MANY WOMEN OFF THE STREETS AND INTO SAFE HOUSING.

BY MICHEAL HALL

MY STORY

I was a single mother raising four children. Motherhood taught me about patience, compassion and empathy. I learned how to enjoy the ride and not be the driver. My children learned how to be grateful for what they had and optimistic about what the future would hold them if they continued to go down the correct pathway. As a single mother, it wasn't easy surviving the storms. My children have witnessed poverty, hunger and unfulfilled needs. I came a long way providing and keeping my children safe. I raised my children in the church and always kept the faith that God would send me a God fearing husband. In March of 2004, God answered my prayers and blessed me with my husband, Roy.

Our family began to grow larger, when we adopted two new additions to the family and had a daughter together in 2007. I became the "Mother Hen". I'm the grandmother of five: three granddaughters, one biological and twin girls who are in my care today, and one grandson . We have a family of fourteen. My mother's wisdom came from Alice Dixson (my Mom). She was my best friend and she is missed dearly. I thank her for all the wisdom and advice that made me the mother, wife and a friend to many. I am the reflection of her mothering style. Her legacy lives on through me. I later met young mothers, in passing, that were in need of help. It seemed like I never meet *strangers*, because when I meet them I feel that God chose me to meet them. They would open up to me with all their troubles and discuss all their problems. I just wasn't able to help them the way I wanted, at that time.

I had to get creative real soon and I discussed a vision with my husband to open a nonprofit organization for homeless mothers. I shared with him my desire to buy property and fixing them up to house homeless mothers that were crying out for help to keep mothers and children safe. My husband agreed and said he thought it was a good idea. I then began to think, What should I name the organization?.... I thought the name: *Charismata* (means a Gift from God) would be a good name.

Charismata Homes opened it's doors in 2009. Charismata Homes has four locations: Westland, Farmington and Detroit. Charismata homes are transitional housing for homeless single mothers facing crises with their children. While in our program , the mothers receive supportive guidance, housing, education, food, clothing and community referrals. We identify the steps to achieve a stable, safe, and secure home for mothers and children. To learn more about our organization, please visit our website below:

www.charismatahomesandcompany.com

FAMILY

LOVE

www.ingramcontent.com/pod-product-compliance
Lightning Source LLC
Chambersburg PA
CBHW040024050426
42452CB00002B/126